monday morning®

ShortCuts
For Early Reading

by Marilynn G. Barr

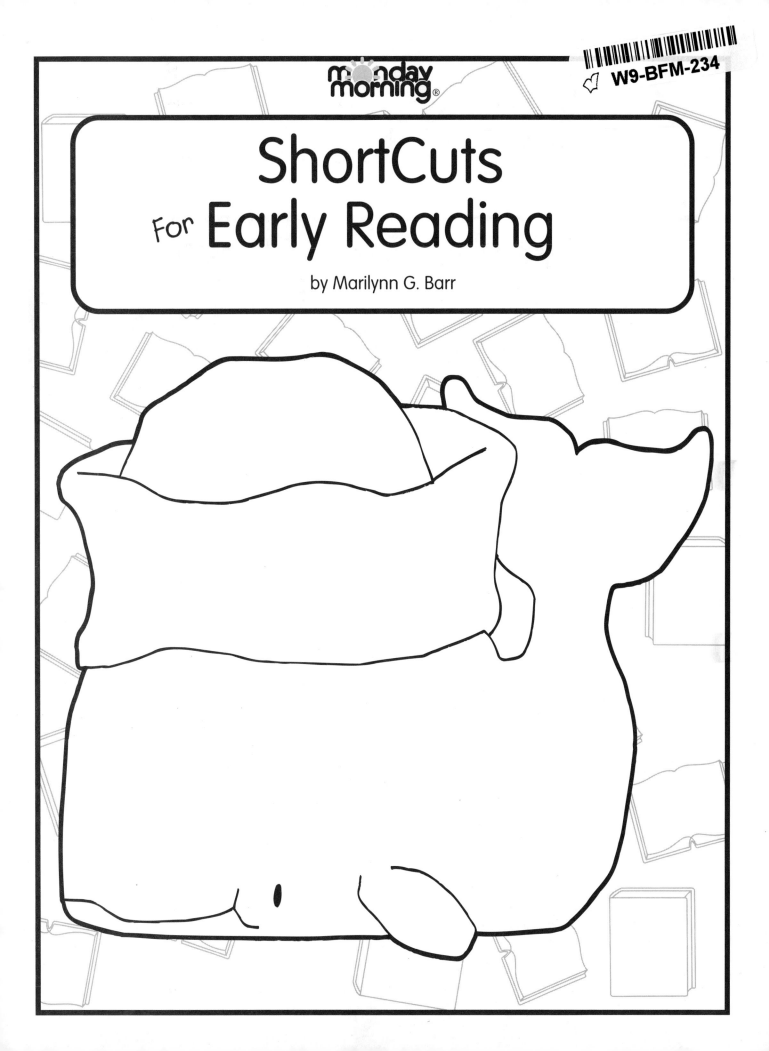

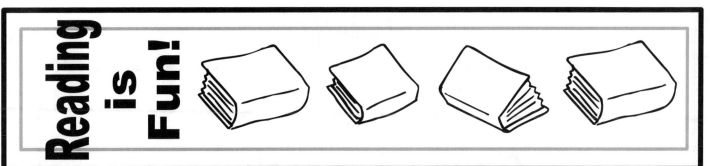

Publisher: Roberta Suid

Production: Little Acorn & Associates, Inc.

MM2221
SHORTCUTS FOR EARLY READING
Entire contents copyright © 2007
by Monday Morning Books, Inc.

For a complete catalog, write to the address below:
Monday Morning Books, Inc.
PO Box 1134
Inverness, CA 94937

Call our toll-free number: 1-800-255-6049
E-mail us at: MMBooks@aol.com
Visit our Web site: http://www.mondaymorningbooks.com
For more products featuring art by Marilynn G. Barr visit www.littleacornbooks.com

monday morning®

ISBN 1-57612-274-3

Printed in the United States of America
9 8 7 6 5 4 3 2 1

Contents

Introduction 4
Sentence Boards 6
Sentence Strips 12
Word Cards
Picture Only Word Cards 17
Picture and Word Cards 22
Word Only Cards 27
Word of the Day Badges 32
Ready, Set, Read 33
Game Boards 34
Story Book Patterns
A Funny Story Book Cover 37
A Funny Story Manuscript Page 38
A True Story Book Cover 39
A True Story Manuscript Page 40
A Silly Story Book Cover 41
A Silly Story Manuscript Page 42
A Super Story Book Cover 43
A Super Story Manuscript Page 44
An Amazing Story Book Cover 45
An Amazing Story Manuscript Page 46
A Wonderful Story Book Cover 47
A Wonderful Story Manuscript Page 48
Awards
Awards Booklet 49
Awards 51

Take-Home Notes 52
Sight Word Cards 53
My New Words 56
Word Lists 57

Introduction

ShortCuts for Early Reading makes early reading skills practice lots of fun. Patterns include Reading Rabbit, Reading Raccoon, Sentence Snail, Sentence Snake, Word Walrus, and Word Whale sentence boards and sentence strips designed to fit on each board. Over 100 beginning, ending, vowel sound, and sight word cards provide children with multiple sentence writing and reading opportunities. Also included are Word of the Day Badges; Ready, Set, Read game; Awards; Take-Home Notes; and My Word List chart for children to keep track of new words.

Sentence Boards

Reproduce, color, and cut out 20 sentence boards (pages 6-11). Reproduce, color, cut out, and glue a sentence strip (pages 12-16) on each sentence board, then laminate. Set up a work station with sentence boards and word cards for children to practice forming sentences. Children can use the *picture only*, *picture and word*, and *word only* cards to form sentences on the sentence boards. Early learners may use the *picture only* cards to form sentences while intermediate and advanced learners may choose to use all three sets of cards to form sentences.

Provide word cards for children to glue on programmed sentence boards to form sentences. Have children decorate construction paper covers. Then help children collate and staple completed sentence boards to form a book.

Reproduce 8 identical sentence boards for each child to form a writing book. Have children color and cut out the sentence boards. Help each child staple boards together to form booklets. Encourage children to write one sentence on each page. Children may choose to write unrelated sentences or sentences that tell a story.

Word Cards

Over 100 cards are included for beginning and ending consonant, consonant blends and digraphs, long and short vowel, and vowel team words. There are three different formats for word cards: *picture only* (pages 17-21), *picture and word* (pages 22-26), and *word only* (pages 27-31). Word cards are designed to use with sentence boards: however, they can also be used to create sentences on plain construction paper sentence strips. Word cards can also double as flash cards for children to practice identifying beginning and ending consonants and long and short vowel sounds.

Reproduce several sets of colored construction paper word cards. Divide the cards into three sets (pictures only, pictures with words, words only). Store each set of cards in a resealable plastic bag.

Word of the Day Badges

Program and reproduce oak tag badges (page 32) with the "Word of the Day" for each child. Have children color and cut out the badges. Use cellophane tape to attach safety pins to the backs of badges for children to wear. Option: Provide each child with a folder. Have children glue badges to the fronts of folders. Write each child's name on the front of the folder. Children can use these folders to store work related to the "Word of the Day" on the cover.

Ready, Set, Read

Children practice reading skills with a rabbit, raccoon, snail, snake, walrus, and whale as they play Ready, Set, Read (pages 33-36).

To play, place a basket of tokens on the table. Then each of two to six players chooses one of the game boards to play. One player shuffles and places the deck of *picture only* word cards (pages 17-21), face down, on the table. Each player, in turn, draws a card, identifies the picture on the card, and places a token on the matching word space on his or her game board. If there is no match, the player places the card, face down, in a discard pile, and the next player takes a turn. Play continues until each player has placed a token on each space on his or her game board. Reshuffle cards to continue play, if needed.

Story Book Patterns

Reproduce a cover and matching writing pages (pages 37-48) for children to create original stories. Early learners may choose to write unrelated sentences while advanced learners might write a series of sentences to tell a "funny, true, silly, or super" story.

Awards

Children love to receive awards as well as keep track of their own achievements. Reproduce award booklets (pages 49-50) for children to color and cut out. Help each child assemble and staple his or her booklet. Store all stickers in a basket. Give children stickers to glue in booklets as they master each listed skill.

Be prepared to reward children for reading skills achievement. Reproduce, color, and cut out a supply of awards (page 51) and store in a decorated awards envelope or folder.

Take-Home Notes

Send home notes (page 52) to keep parents informed about current reading skills practice. Reproduce and cut apart a supply of bright-colored paper notes. Store notes in a decorated manila envelope or folder.

Sight Word Cards

Reproduce and glue sight word cards (pages 53-55) to the back of a sheet of gift wrap, then laminate, and cut apart the cards. Use these cards as flash cards. Help children identify the first letter as well as the first, middle, or ending sounds for each sight word.

Reproduce several sets of construction paper sight word cards. Store cards in a resealable plastic bag. Prepare a work station with sentence strips, sheets of construction paper, and four containers filled with words cards (*sight words, picture only, picture and word,* and *word only* cards). Children can work in two person teams to glue word cards on sentence strips or create sentences by gluing cards on a sheet of construction paper. Post finished work on a display board entitled "See What We Wrote!"

Note: All word cards including sight word cards are designed to fit on sentence strips.

My New Words

Reproduce a My New Words chart (page 56) for each child. Have children color, cut out, and glue charts on a sheet of construction paper. Encourage children to list new words they learn while at home or in school. Invite each child to share new words.

Sentence Board

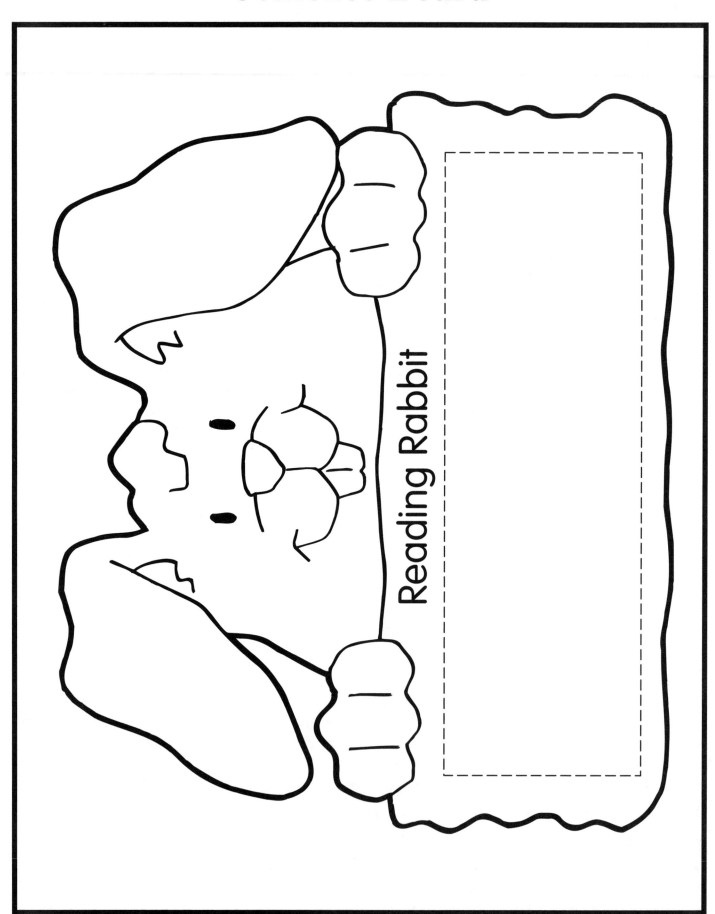

Reading Rabbit

Sentence Board

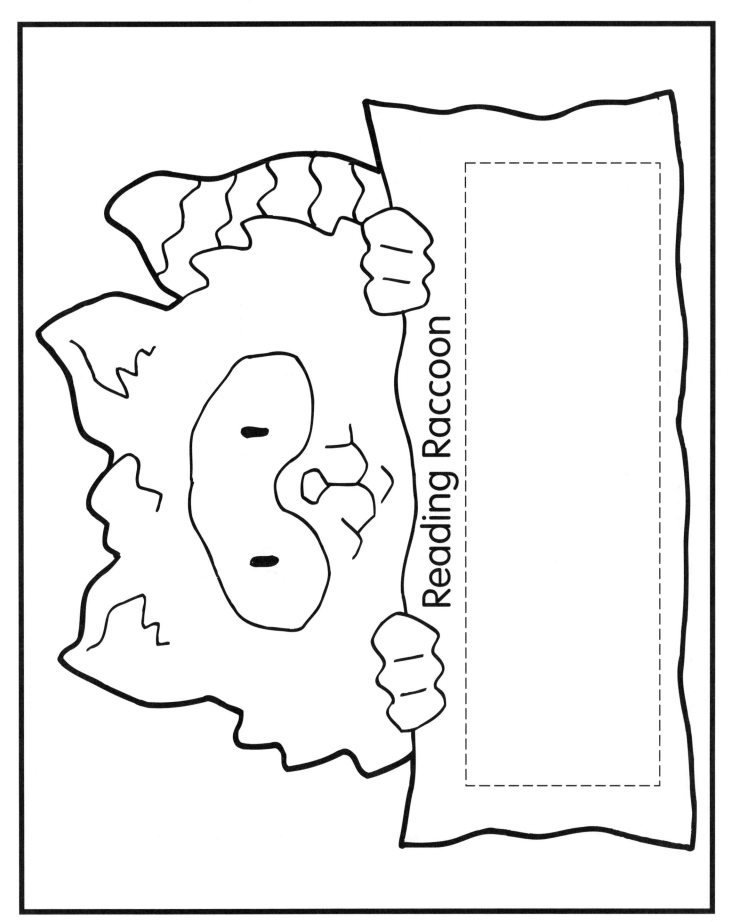

Reading Raccoon

Sentence Board

Sentence Snail

Sentence Board

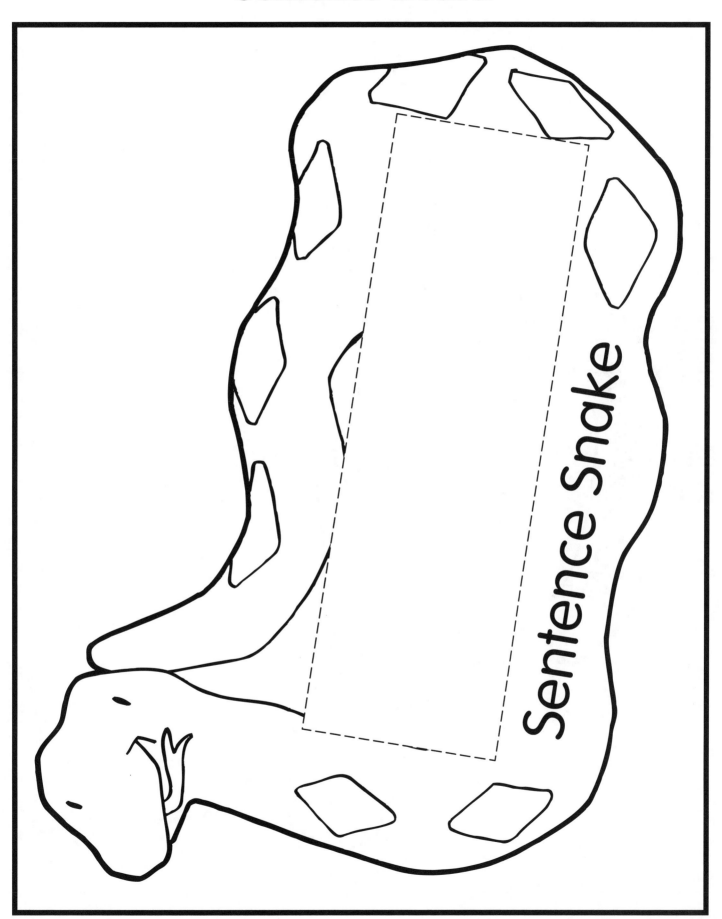

Sentence Snake

Sentence Board

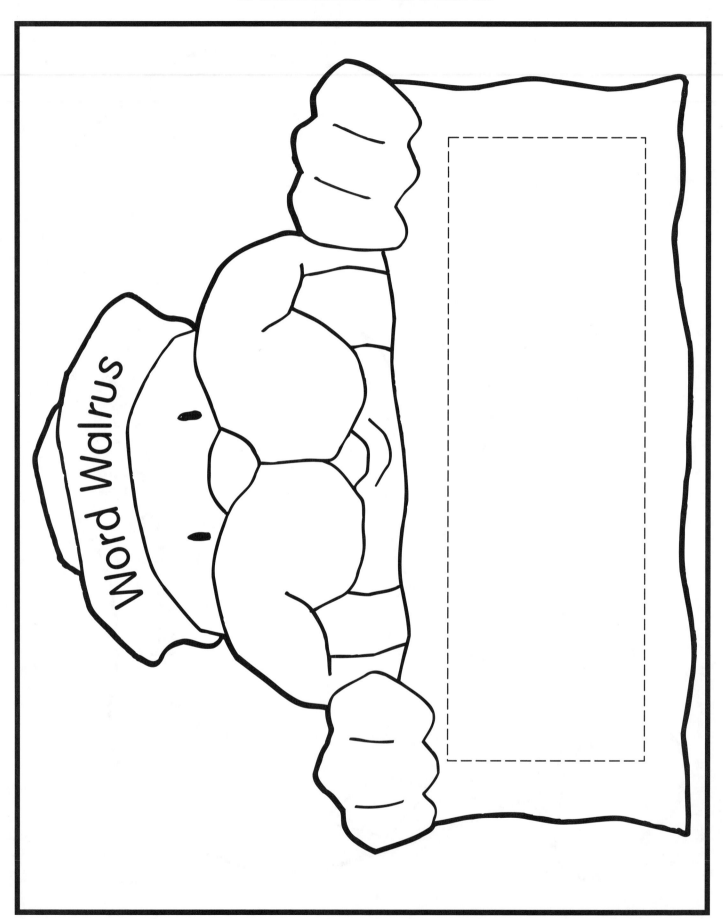

10

Sentence Board

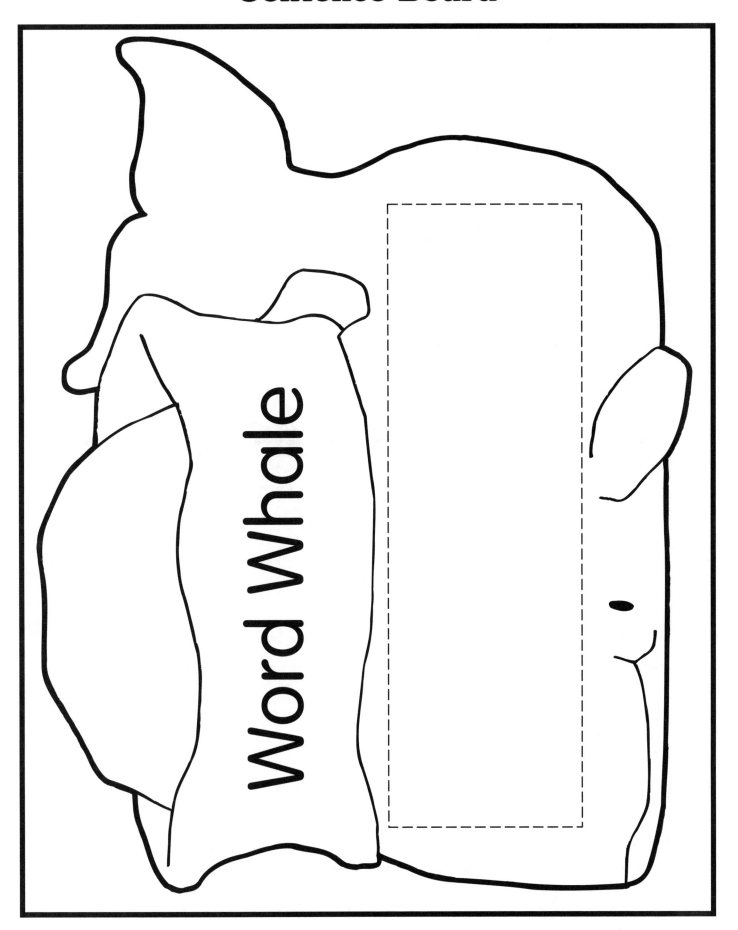

Word Whale

Sentence Strips

I see a ☐ .

I do not see a ☐ .

I see an ☐ .

I do not see an ☐ .

12

Sentence Strips

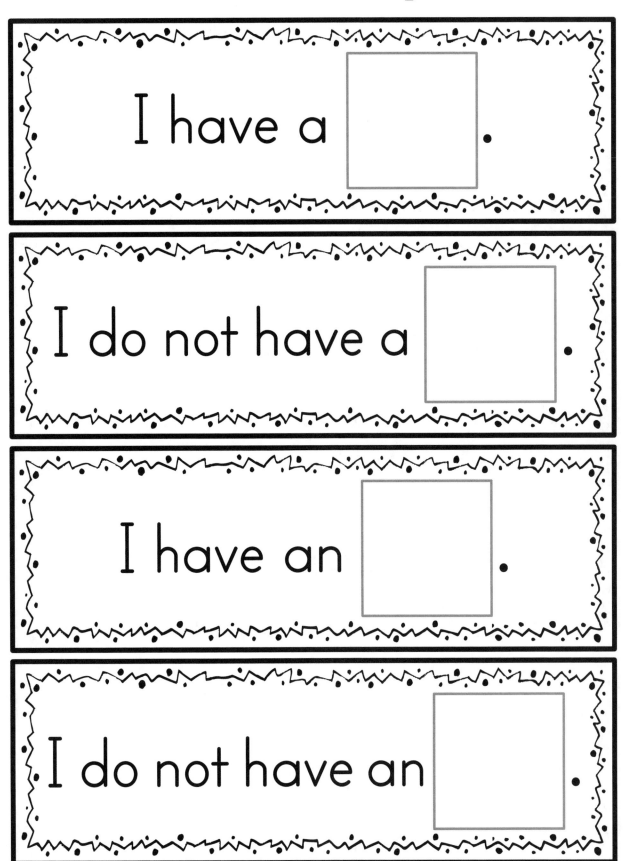

I have a ☐ .

I do not have a ☐ .

I have an ☐ .

I do not have an ☐ .

Sentence Strips

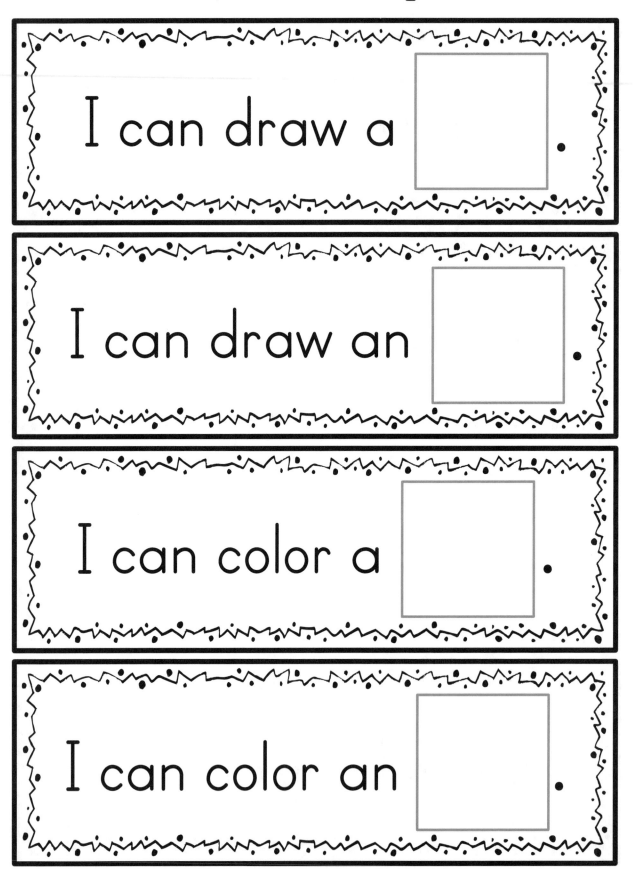

I can draw a ☐.

I can draw an ☐.

I can color a ☐.

I can color an ☐.

Sentence Strips

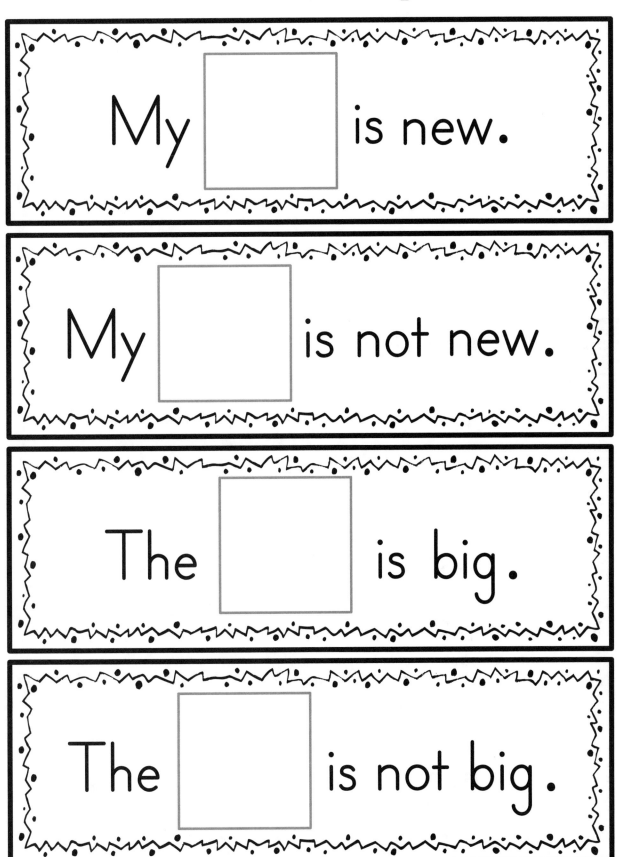

My ☐ is new.

My ☐ is not new.

The ☐ is big.

The ☐ is not big.

Sentence Strips

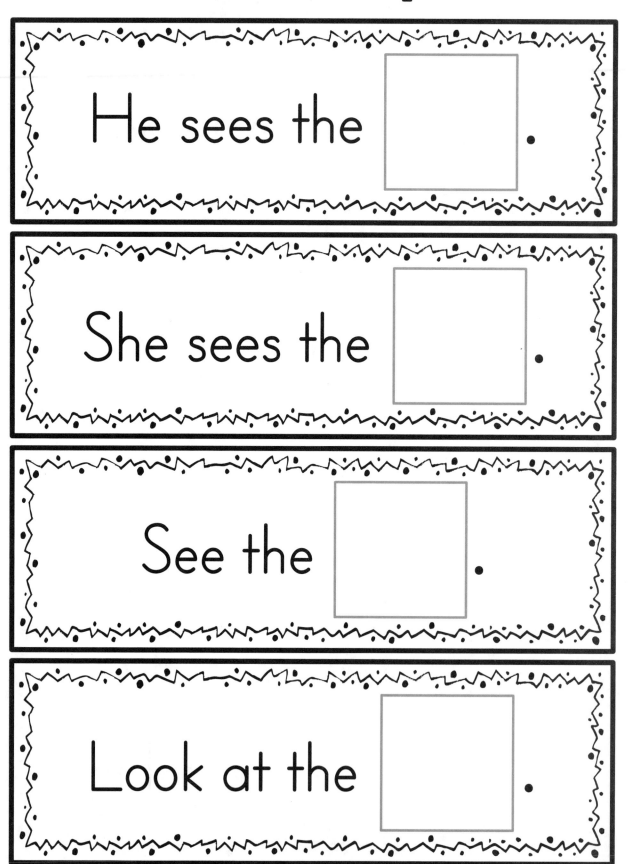

He sees the ☐.

She sees the ☐.

See the ☐.

Look at the ☐.

Picture Only Word Cards

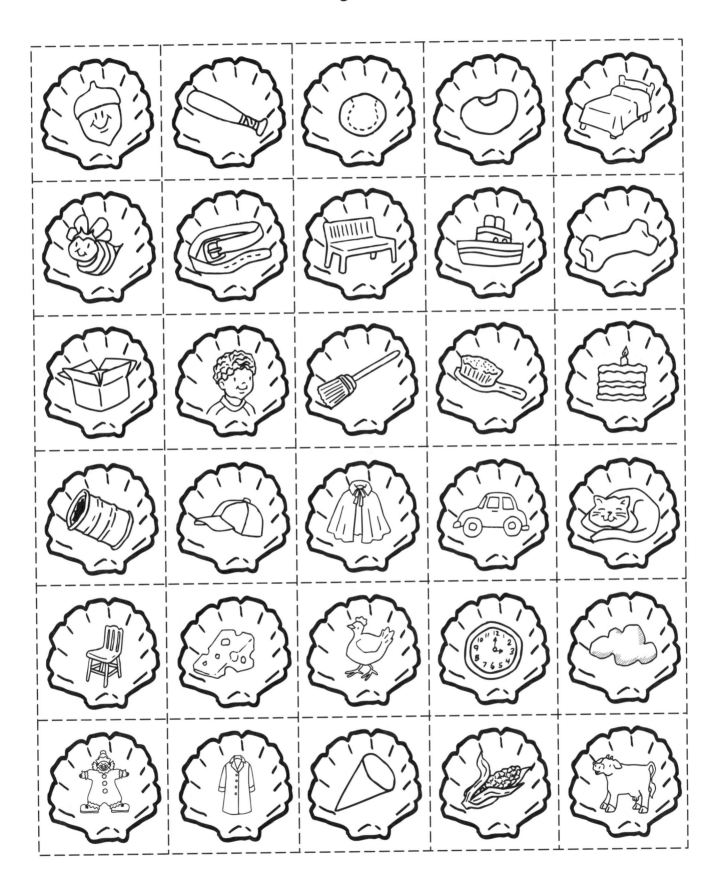

Picture Only Word Cards

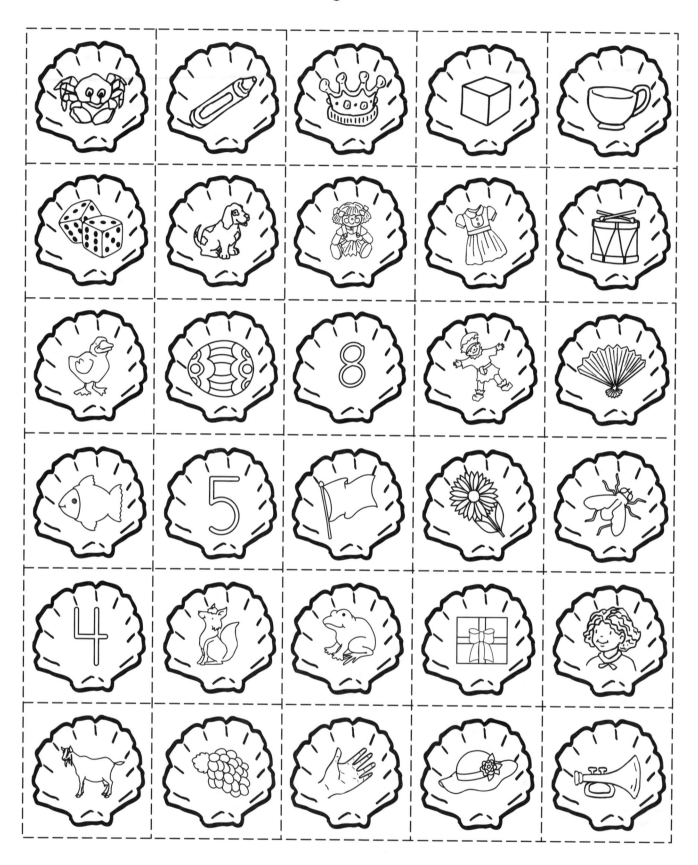

Picture Only Word Cards

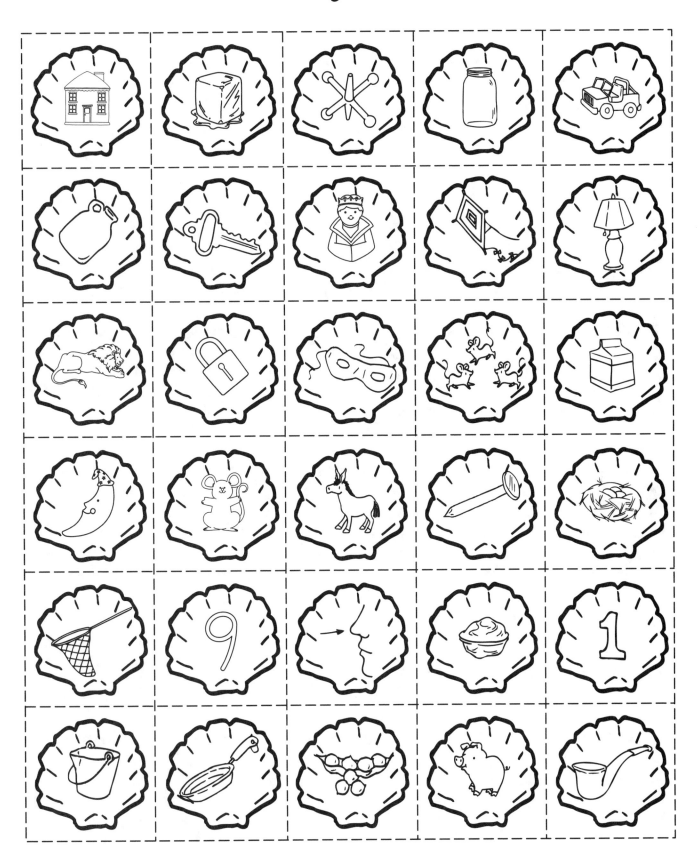

Picture Only Word Cards

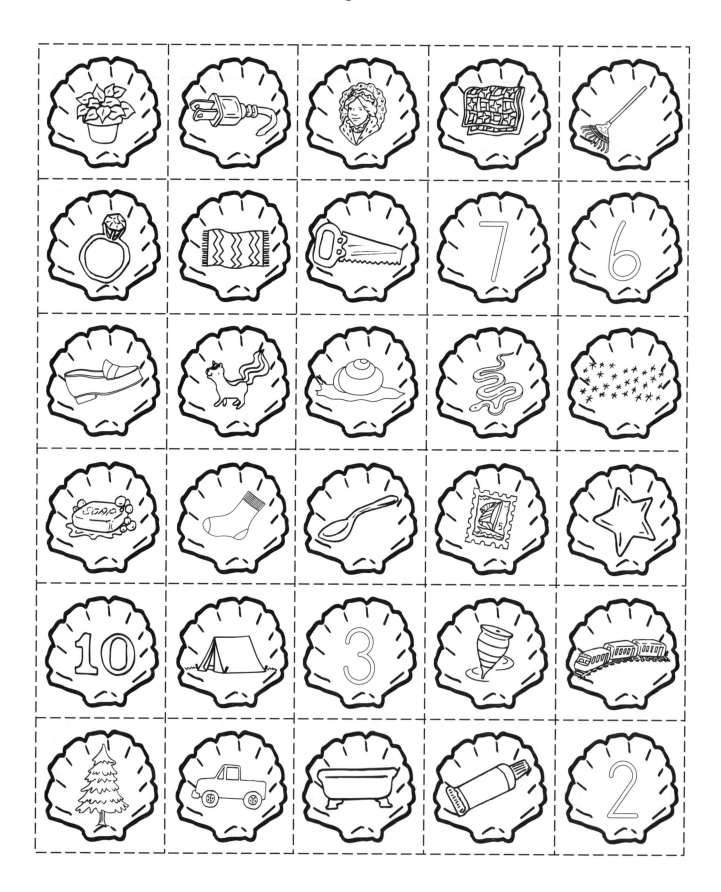

Picture Only Word Cards

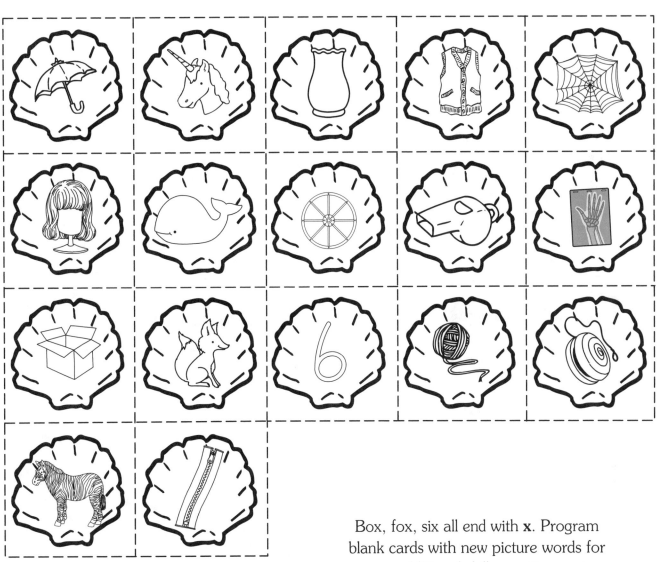

Box, fox, six all end with **x**. Program blank cards with new picture words for additional skills practice.

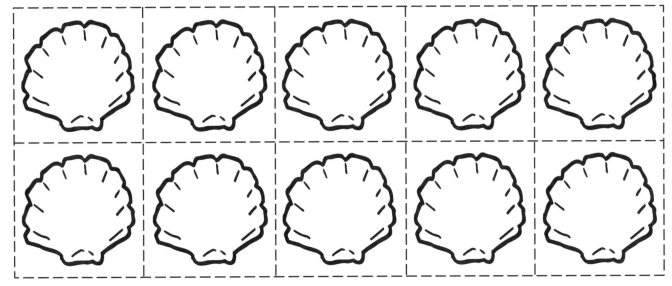

Picture and Word Cards

acorn	bat	ball	bean	bed
bee	belt	bench	boat	bone
box	boy	broom	brush	cake
can	cap	cape	car	cat
chair	cheese	chicken	clock	cloud
clown	coat	cone	corn	cow

Picture and Word Cards

crab	crayon	crown	cube	cup
dice	dog	doll	dress	drum
duck	egg	eight	elf	fan
fish	five	flag	flower	fly
four	fox	frog	gift	girl
goat	grapes	hand	hat	horn

Picture and Word Cards

house	ice	jack	jar	jeep
jug	key	king	kite	lamp
lion	lock	mask	mice	milk
moon	mouse	mule	nail	nest
net	nine	nose	nut	one
pail	pan	peas	pig	pipe

Picture and Word Cards

plant plug queen quilt rake

ring rug saw 7 seven 6 six

shoe skunk snail snake snow

soap sock spoon stamp star

10 ten tent 3 three top train

tree truck tub tube 2 two

Picture and Word Cards

umbrella

unicorn

vase

vest

web

wig

whale

wheel

whistle

x-ray

box

fox

six

yarn

yo-yo

zebra

zipper

Box, fox, six all end with **x**.
Program blank cards with new pictures
and words for additional skills practice.

Word Only Cards

acorn	bat	ball	bean	bed
bee	belt	bench	boat	bone
box	boy	broom	brush	cake
can	cap	cape	car	cat
chair	cheese	chicken	clock	cloud
clown	coat	cone	corn	cow

Word Cards

crab	crayon	crown	cube	cup
dice	dog	doll	dress	drum
duck	egg	eight	elf	fan
fish	five	flag	flower	fly
four	fox	frog	gift	girl
goat	grapes	hand	hat	horn

Word Cards

house	ice	jack	jar	jeep
jug	key	king	kite	lamp
lion	lock	mask	mice	milk
moon	mouse	mule	nail	nest
net	nine	nose	nut	one
pail	pan	peas	pig	pipe

Word Cards

plant	plug	queen	quilt	rake
ring	rug	saw	seven	six
shoe	skunk	snail	snake	snow
soap	sock	spoon	stamp	star
ten	tent	three	top	train
tree	truck	tub	tube	two

Word Cards

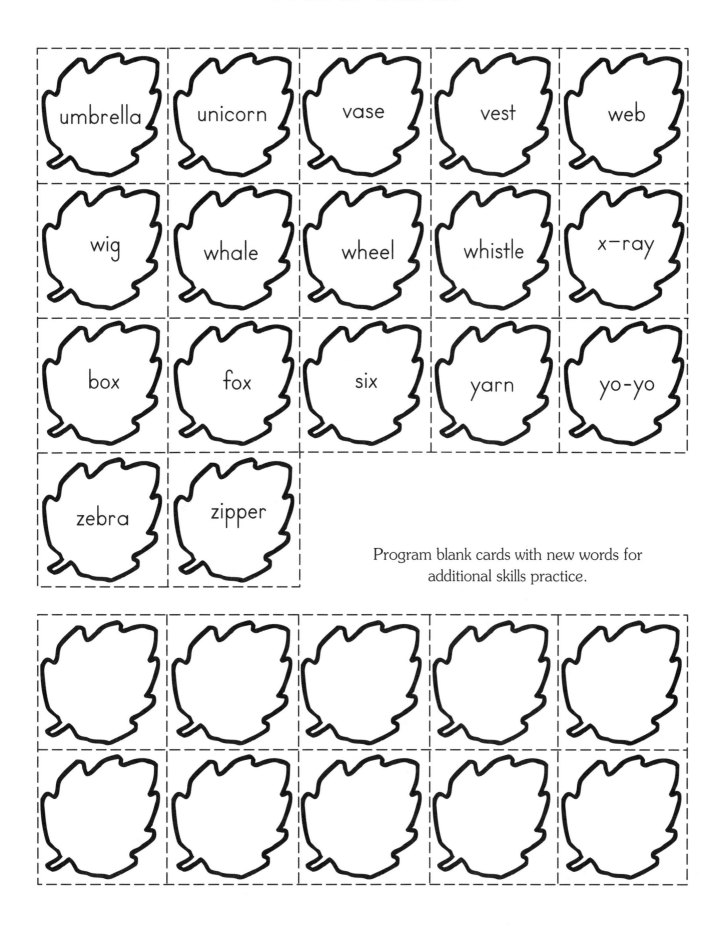

umbrella	unicorn	vase	vest	web
wig	whale	wheel	whistle	x-ray
box	fox	six	yarn	yo-yo
zebra	zipper			

Program blank cards with new words for additional skills practice.

Word of the Day Badges

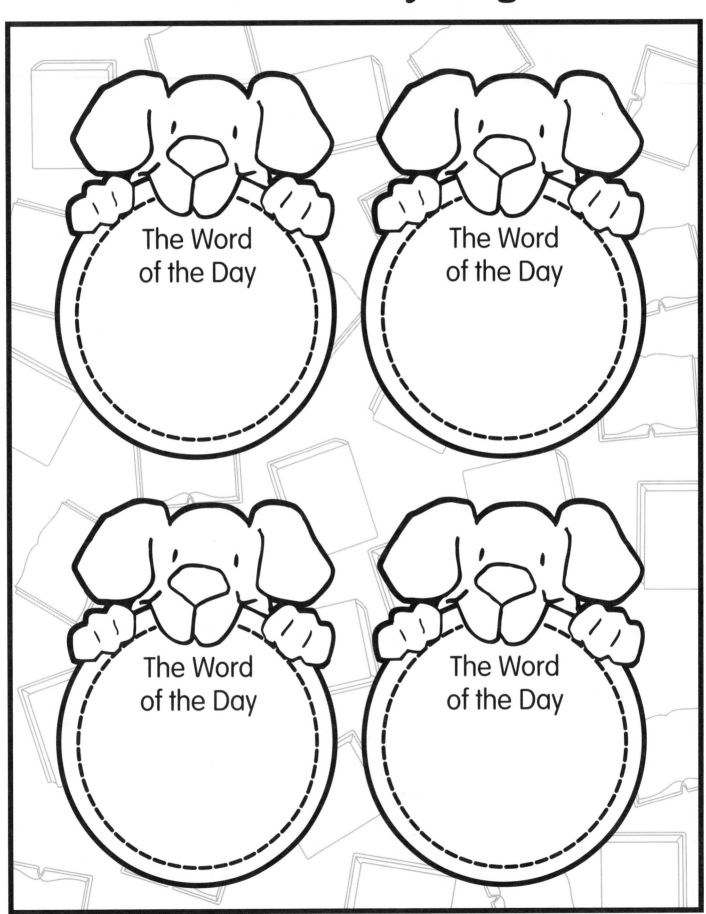

The Word of the Day

The Word of the Day

The Word of the Day

The Word of the Day

Ready, Set, Read

Reproduce, color, and cut out the game board patterns, tokens, and picture only word cards (pages 17-21). Glue each game board pattern to a sheet of oak tag or construction paper. Laminate the game boards and game cards. Cut out the tokens and game cards. Decorate a manila envelope to store the game boards and cards. Option: Reproduce, color, and glue each page of game cards to the back of a sheet of gift wrap, then laminate and cut out the cards.

Tokens

Reproduce six sets of tokens.

Ready, Set, Read Game Boards

ball	nest	mice	jack	fan	broom
yarn	bean	nine	mule	bench	jug
chicken	nail	dog	dress	plant	tub
tube	bed			peas	brush

horn	whale	queen	crab	ring	hat
jug	cap	box	skunk	bee	cheese
lion	wig	nut	soap	whistle	ten
clock	ten			star	rake

Ready, Set, Read Game Boards

ball	clown	boy	goat	king	clock
shoe	brush	kite	vest	cat	nose
gift	mask	snow	bat	cup	quilt
train	spoon			zipper	flower

key	flag	fish	drum	can	six
pan	cake	truck	lamp	x-ray	pail
dog	dice	zebra	stamp	belt	top
frog	three			crayon	elf

Ready, Set, Read Game Cards

rug	car	fly	jar	hat	cloud
shoe	goat	moon	bed	duck	chair
pig	cube	vase	yo-yo	boat	cape
plug	web			tub	cube

fox	milk	snake	net	grapes	cone
king	bone	wheel	girl	jeep	plug
pig	coat	web	corn	lock	sock
tent	egg			crown	doll

A Funny Story Book Cover

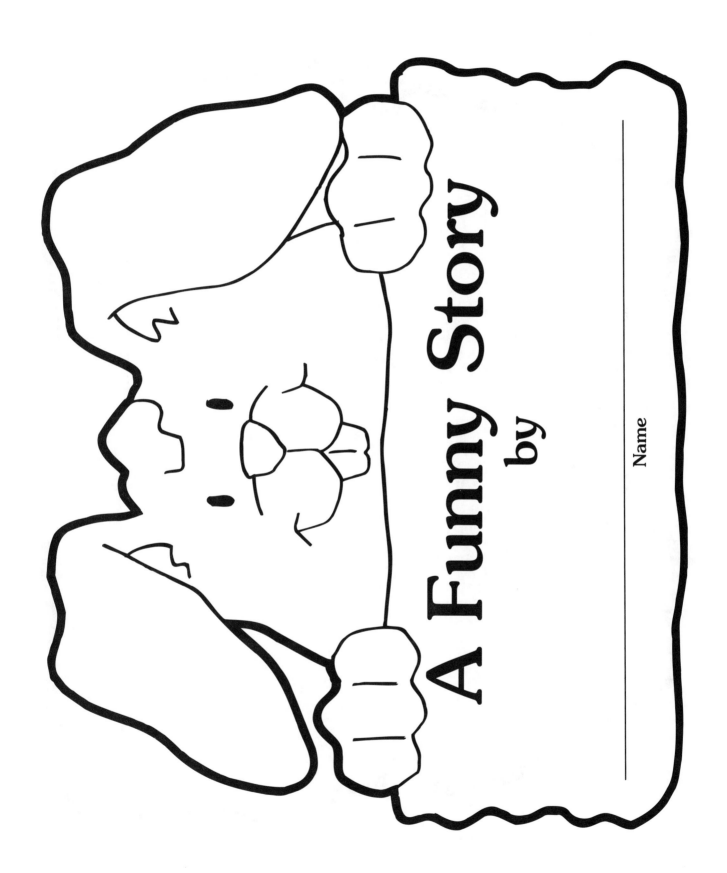

A Funny Story Manuscript Page

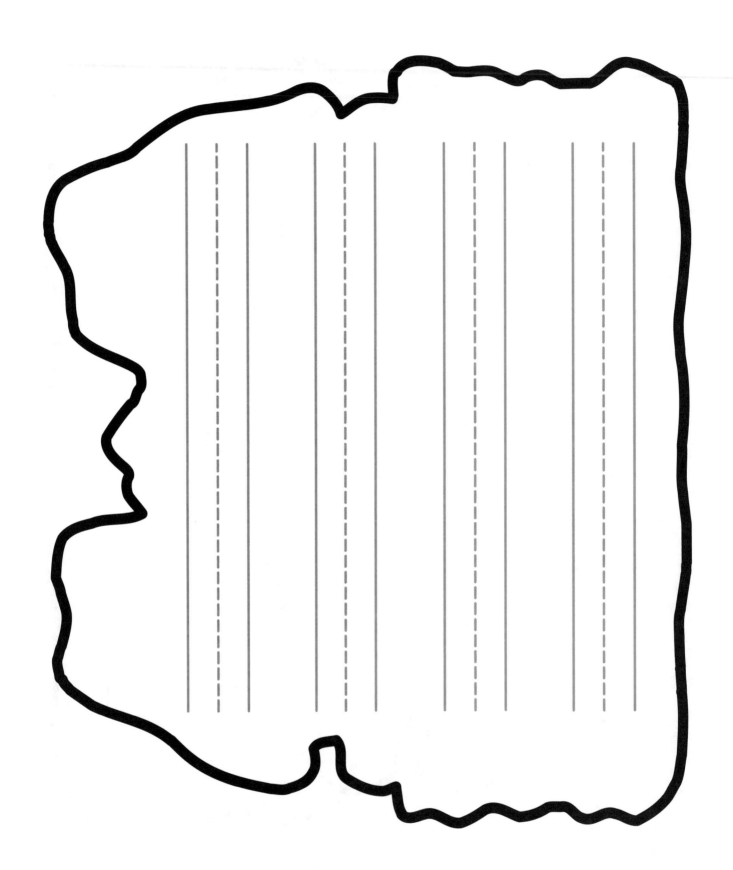

A True Story Book Cover

A True Story by

Name

A True Story Manuscript Page

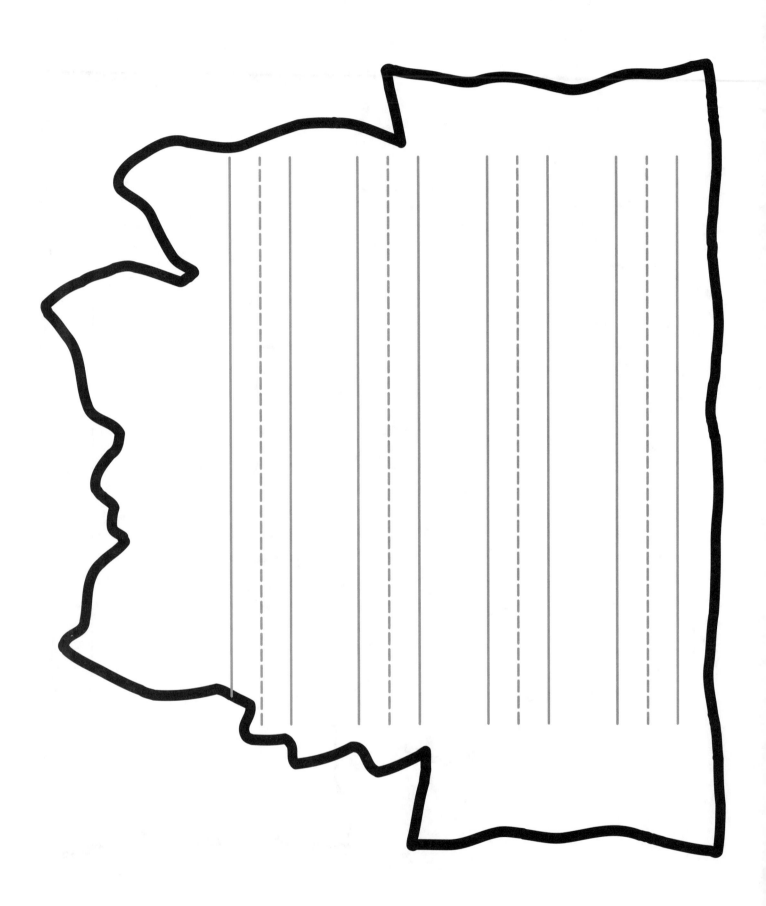

A Silly Story Book Cover

A Silly Story
by

_____
Name

A Silly Story Manuscript Page

A Super Story Book Cover

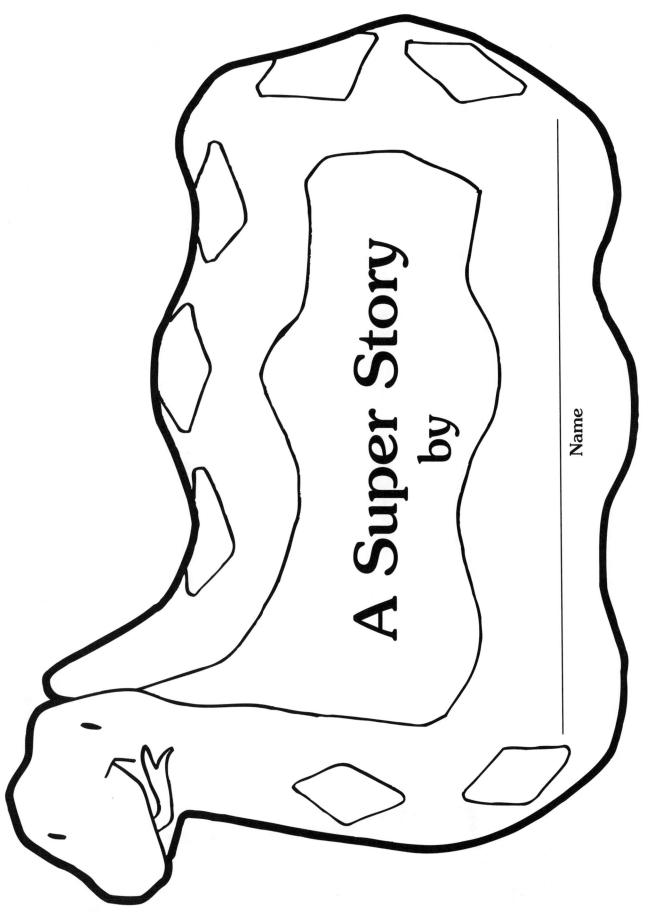

A Super Story by

Name

A Super Story Manuscript Page

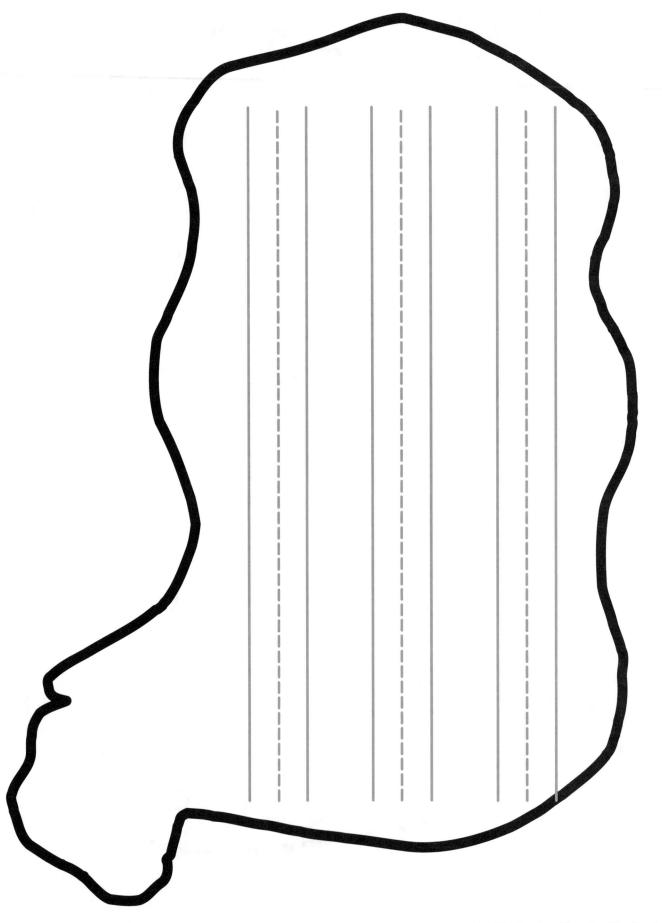

An Amazing Story Book Cover

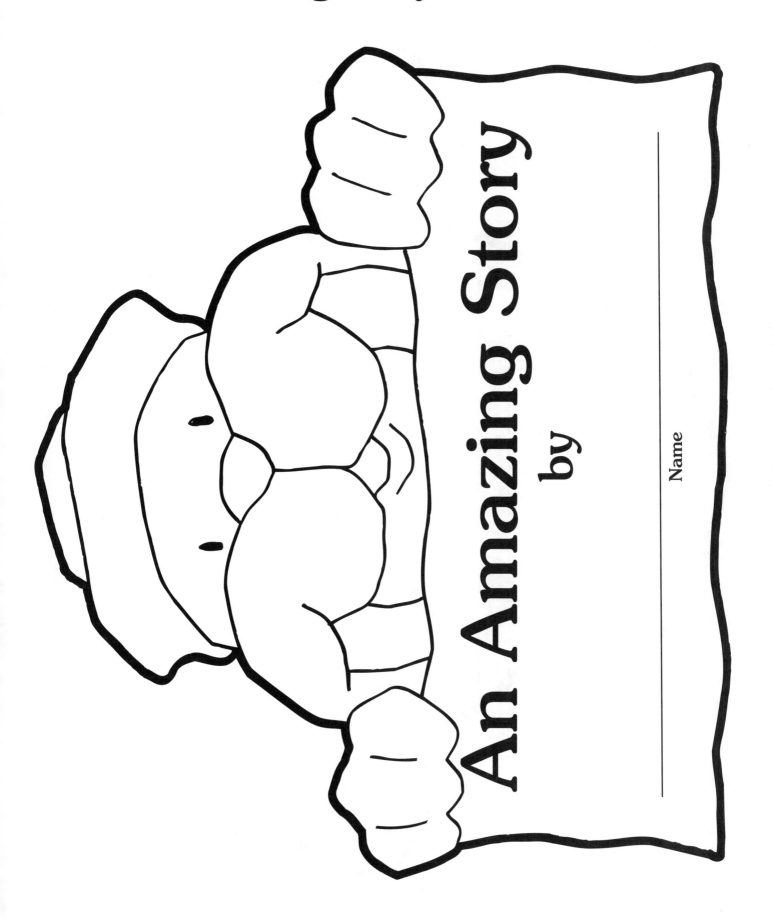

An Amazing Story
by

Name

An Amazing Story Manuscript Page

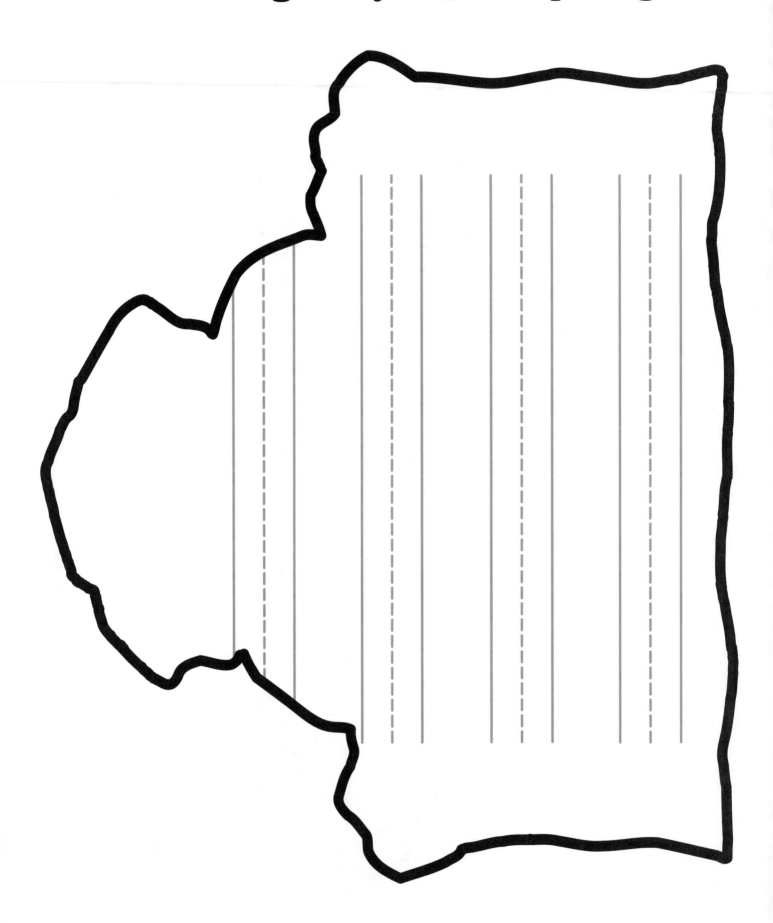

A Wonderful Story Book Cover

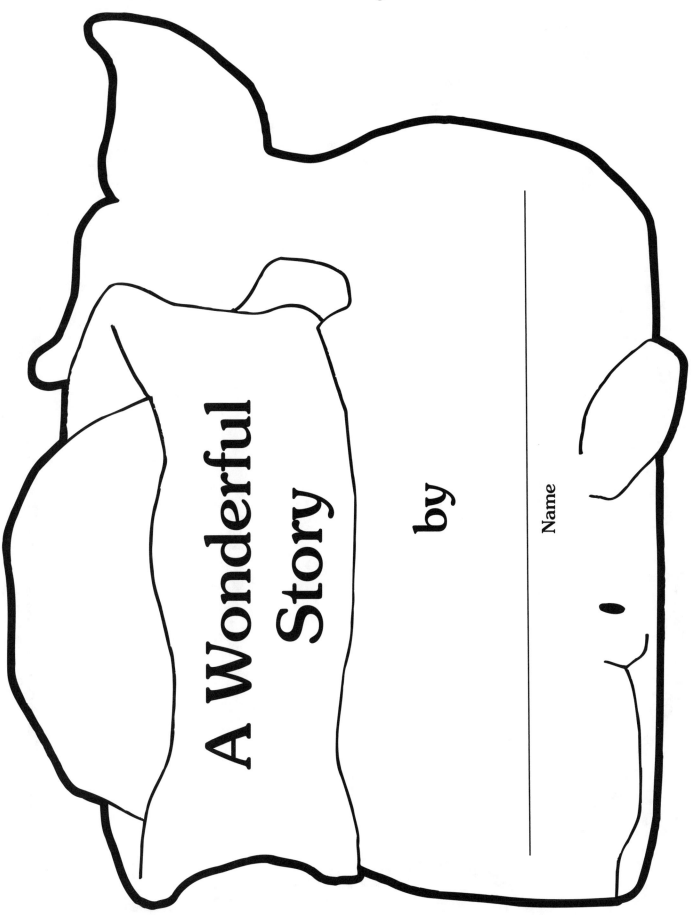

A Wonderful Story

by

Name

A Wonderful Story Manuscript Page

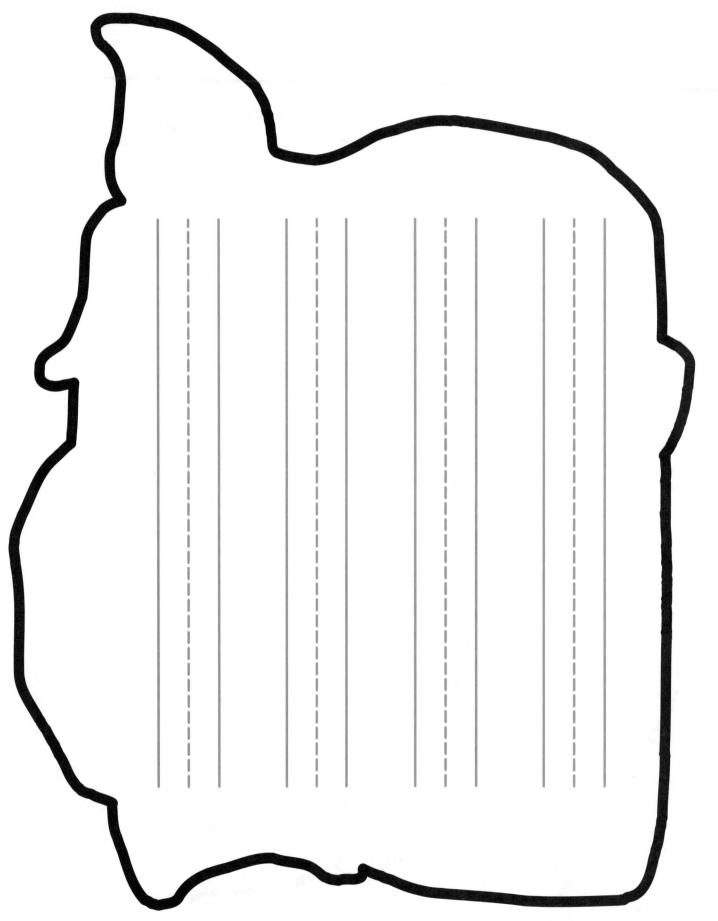

Awards Booklet

I can read.

Glue a Good Job! sticker here.

I can read sight words.

Glue a Good Job! sticker here.

My Reading Awards Booklet

Good Job!

I can read number words.

Glue a Good Job! sticker here.

Awards Booklet

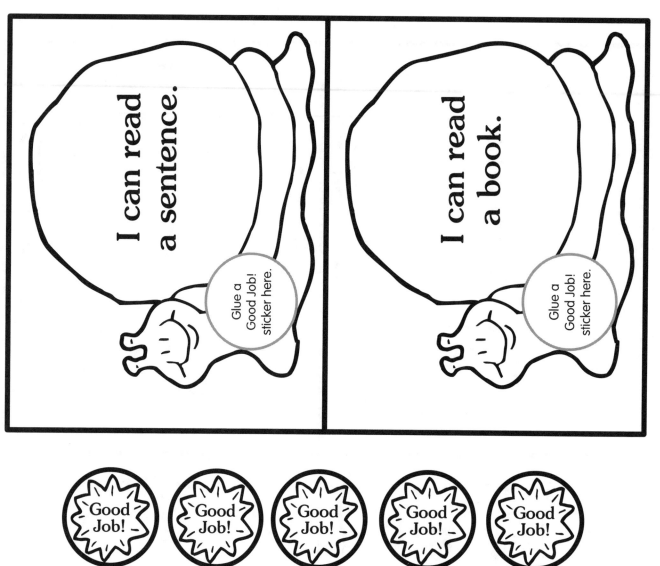

Awards

is an
Excellent Reader!

Name

Teacher

is a
Really Good Reader!

Name

Teacher

is a
Speedy Reader.

Name

Teacher

is a
Super Reader.

Name

Teacher

Take-Home Notes

Good Books
to Read!

Dear Parent,
We are learning to read.
Please help your child learn
the words listed below.

Teacher

Sight Word Cards

a	all	am	and	are
at	ate	away	be	big
but	came	can	color	come
cut	did	do	down	eat
find	five	for	four	funny
go	glue	has	have	he

Sight Word Cards

her	hers	his	hot	I
if	in	into	is	it
jump	like	little	look	make
me	must	my	new	nine
no	not	now	on	one
our	out	play	please	ran

Sight Word Cards

run	said	saw	say	see
she	so	soon	that	the
them	there	they	these	too
two	under	up	we	well
went	what	who	will	with
yes	you			

Program blank cards with new sight words for additional skills practice.

My New Words

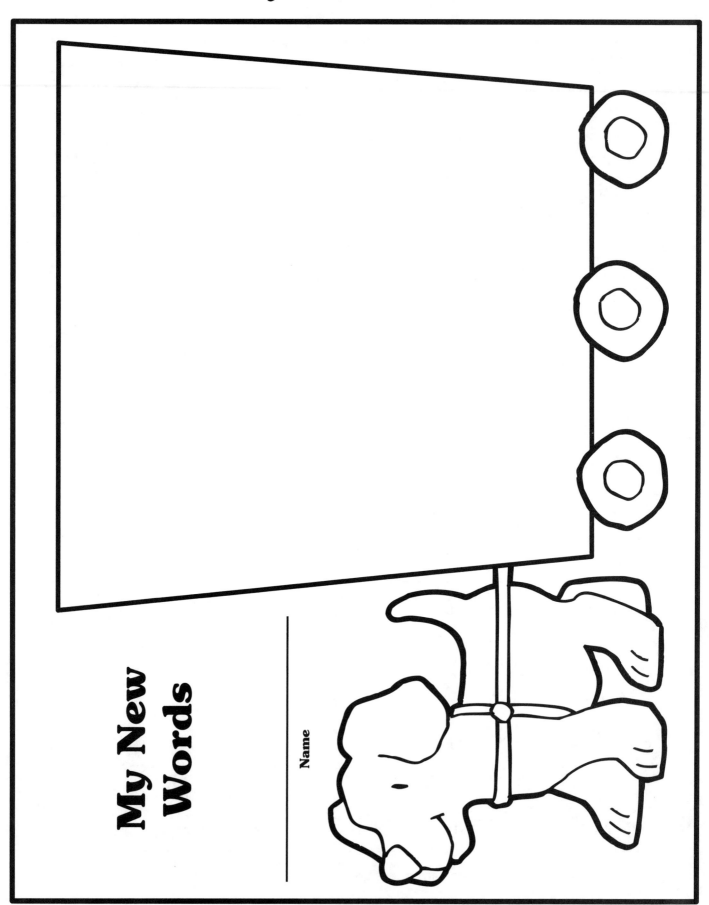

My New
Words

Name

Word List

Beginning Consonant Words

New Words

_____

_____

_____

_____

_____

_____

_____

b	**d**	**m**	**s**
ball	dice	mask	six
bat	dog	mice	soap
bean	doll	milk	sock
bee	duck	moon	**t**
bed	**f**	mule	ten
belt	fan	**n**	tent
bench	fish	nail	top
boat	fox	nest	tub
bone	frog	net	tube
box	**g**	nine	**v**
boy	gift	nose	vase
brush	girl	nut	vest
c	goat	**p**	**w**
cake	**h**	pail	web
can	hat	pan	wig
car	horn	peas	**x**
cap	**j**	pig	x-ray
cape	jack	**qu**	**y**
cat	jar	queen	yarn
clock	jeep	quilt	yo-yo
coat	jug	**r**	**z**
cone	**k**	rake	zebra
corn	key	ring	zipper
cube	king	rug	
cup	kite		
	l		
	lamp		
	lion		
	lock		

Word List

Beginning Consonant Blend Words

bl	**dr**	**sk**	**New Words**
black	dress	skunk	_____
blue	drum	**sn**	_____
br	**fl**	snake	_____
brown	flower	snow	_____
broom	flag	**sp**	_____
brush	fly	spoon	_____
cl	**gr**	**sq**	_____
clock	grapes	square	_____
clown	green	**st**	_____
cloud	**pl**	star	_____
cr	plant	stamp	_____
crab	plug	**tr**	
crayon		truck	
crown		train	

Beginning Consonant Digraph Words

ch	**th**	**New Words**
chair	three	_____
cheese	**wh**	_____
chicken	whale	_____
sh	white	_____
shoe	wheel	_____
	whistle	_____
		_____
		_____

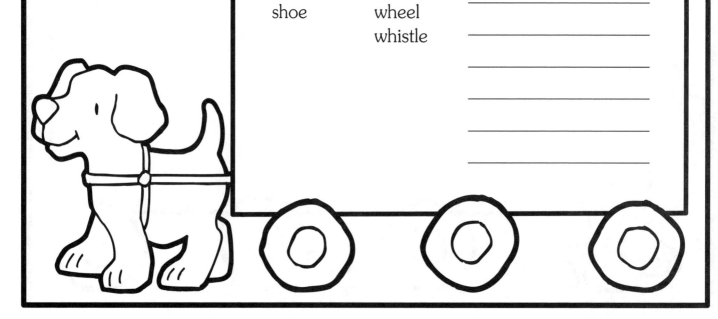

Word List

Ending Consonant Words

b	n	p	t
tub	brown	cap	bat
web	can	cup	cat
d	clown	jeep	coat
bed	corn	lamp	eight
red	fan	top	goat
f	green	**r**	hat
elf	horn	car	net
g	lion	jar	nest
dog	moon	star	nut
egg	pan	zipper	tent
jug	queen		vest
king	seven		**x**
plug	spoon		box
pig	sun		six
l	ten		fox
ball	train		
doll	unicorn		
girl	violin		
nail	yarn		
pail			
snail			

New Words

_____

_____

_____

_____

_____

_____

_____

_____

Word List

Ending Consonant Blend Words

ft	gift
lf	elf
lk	milk
lt	belt, quilt
ng	king
mp	lamp
nt	tent
sk	mask
st	nest, vest

New Words

_____
_____
_____
_____
_____
_____
_____
_____
_____

Ending Consonant Digraph Words

ch	**sh**
bench	fish
ck	brush
black	
clock	
duck	
jack	
lock	
sock	
truck	

New Words

_____
_____
_____
_____
_____
_____
_____
_____
_____

Word List

Long Vowel Words

a	e	i	o	u
acorn	bean	dice	boat	cube
cake	bee	five	bone	mule
cape	jeep	ice	coat	tube
nail	key	kite	cone	unicorn
pail	tree	lion	goat	
rake	peas	mice	nose	
snail	queen	nine	soap	
snake	zebra	pipe	snow	
vase		white	yo-yo	
whale				

New Words

_____   _____

_____   _____

_____   _____

_____   _____

_____   _____

_____   _____

_____   _____

_____   _____

Word List

Short Vowel Words

a	e	i	o	u
bat	bed	fish	box	brush
black	belt	gift	clock	cup
can	bench	king	doll	drum
cap	dress	milk	fox	duck
cat	egg	pig	frog	jug
crab	eight	ring	lock	nut
fan	elf	six	sock	plug
flag	net	wig	top	rug
hat	red	zipper		sun
jack	seven			truck
lamp	ten			tub
plant	tent			
stamp	vest			
	web			

New Words

_____   _____

_____   _____

_____   _____

_____   _____

_____   _____

_____   _____

_____   _____

Word List

Rhyming Sets

bat, cat, hat
bee, key, tree
bone, cone
boat, coat, goat
can, fan, pan
car, jar, star
corn, horn
duck, truck
box, fox
dice, ice, mice
clock, lock, sock
nest, vest
nail, pail, snail, whale
pig, wig

New Words

_____   _____

_____   _____

_____   _____

_____   _____

_____   _____

_____   _____

_____   _____

Word List

Sight Words

a	has	play
all	have	please
am	he	ran
and	her	run
are	hers	said
at	his	saw
ate	hot	say
away	I	see
be	if	she
big	in	so
but	into	soon
came	is	that
can	it	the
color	jump	them
come	like	there
cut	little	they
did	look	these
do	make	too
down	me	two
eat	must	under
find	my	up
five	new	we
for	nine	well
four	no	went
funny	not	what
go	now	who
glue	on	will
	one	with
	our	yes
	out	you

New Words

_____

_____

_____

_____

_____

_____

_____

_____

_____

_____

_____

_____

_____

_____

_____

_____

_____

_____

_____

_____